MW00981226

What's the Water Cycle?

Working in a Loop

Ava Beasley

COMPUTER KIDS
Powered by Computational Thinking

PowerKiDS
press.

Published in 2018 by The Rosen Publishing Group, Inc.
29 East 21st Street, New York, NY 10010

Book Design: Jennifer Ryder-Talbot
Editor: Caitie McAneney

Photo Credits: Cover Muhamad hamizi sharif/Shutterstock.com; p. 4 Mykola Mazuryk/
Shutterstock.com; p. 4 (diagram) Merkushev Vasiliy/Shutterstock.com; p. 4, 7, 8, 11,
12, 15, 16, 19, 20 (weather icons) A_KUDR/Shutterstock.com; p. 7 Ovchinnikova Irina/
Shutterstock.com; p. 8 patjo/Shutterstock.com; p. 11 Dr Morley Read/Shutterstock.com;
p. 12-13 dachnarong wangkeeree/Shutterstock.com; p. 15 Singkham/Shutterstock.com; p.
16 (main) Africa Studio/Shutterstock.com; p. 16 (hail) Suzanne Tucker/Shutterstock.com; p.
19 Sundry Photography/Shutterstock.com; p. 21 viktori-art/Shutterstock.com.

Library of Congress Cataloging-in-Publication Data
Names: Beasley, Ava.
Title: What's the water cycle?: working in a loop / Ava Beasley.
Description: New York : Rosen Classroom, 2018. | Series: Computer Kids: Powered by
Computational Thinking | Includes glossary and index.
Identifiers: LCCN ISBN 9781538353134 (pbk.) | ISBN 9781538324455 (library bound) |
ISBN 9781538355343 (6pack) | ISBN 9781508137412 (ebook)
Subjects: LCSH: Hydrologic cycle--Juvenile literature. | Water--Juvenile literature.
Classification: LCC GB662.3 B43 2018 | DDC 551.48--dc23

Manufactured in the United States of America

CPSIA Compliance Information: Batch #WS18RC: For Further Information contact Rosen Publishing, New York, New York at 1-800-237-9932

Table of Contents

This **diagram** shows how water moves from the ground to the sky, and falls back to the ground again. The arrows show how it is a loop.

Water, Water, Everywhere

Earth is the only planet in our **solar system** that is known to support life. That's because Earth has water. Water covers more than 70 percent of Earth's surface and it moves in a constant cycle.

A cycle is a **series** of events that happen over and over again. The same things happen every cycle. The water cycle is a series of events in which water passes from Earth's surface to the sky and back again. The water moves in a loop pattern. Because of that, we know what will happen to water from one step to the next. Let's follow the water cycle!

Starting the Cycle

Have you ever visited the ocean? The ocean is the largest body of water in the world. It is home to many kinds of fish and **marine** animals. Other bodies of water include lakes, rivers, and streams. Creeks, ponds, and puddles are smaller collections of water. Groundwater is found in the soil and in places between rocks and sand. Bodies of water and groundwater are our starting point in the water cycle.

Water can exist in solid, liquid, and gas form. The water in this part of the cycle is liquid. It's about to go through a big change!

There are five oceans on Earth, but many people consider them to be one large ocean.

You can see water evaporating when cool air meets warm water. This happens in volcanic lakes or even hot tubs.

Turning into Vapor

The gas form of water is called water vapor. When water turns from liquid to gas, it's called evaporation. This often happens when the temperature rises. Sometimes you can feel the water vapor in the air. The air may feel heavy. That's called humidity.

You can see evaporation if you watch a puddle in the sun. Over time, the puddle will start to dry up. You may notice dew on leaves in the morning that goes away by afternoon. That's evaporation, too. The tiny droplets of water vapor float up into the air.

Plants Transpire

Water vapor doesn't only come from bodies of water. It also comes from plants. Plants take in water from the soil through their roots. Water travels up the roots to the stem, and from the stem to the leaves. Each leaf has many **pores** on it. The pores are so small we can't see them. The water comes out through the pores and turns into water vapor.

How can you test transpiration? Put a clear plastic bag over a healthy potted plant. Over time, you'll notice tiny water droplets form in the bag, which would have escaped into the **atmosphere**.

You can see the water vapor hanging around the trees in this rain forest. There are many trees transpiring in a rain forest.

Up in the Clouds

Water vapor floats up into the atmosphere. Rising air currents take the vapor high into the sky. The vapor comes together and turns back into tiny liquid water droplets. When the water turns from gas to liquid, that's called condensation.

These clouds are small and white, and droplets won't be heavy enough to fall.

When many droplets come together, they form clouds. Some clouds are wispy and white, while other clouds are heavy and gray. Wind moves clouds from one place to another. You may have noticed that not all cloudy days are rainy. That's because not all clouds produce rain. However, if the water droplets become heavy enough, then they will fall to the ground.

What Is Precipitation?

When water falls to the ground, it's called precipitation. That's the next step in the water cycle. Precipitation falls as rain if temperatures are warm enough. Some rain comes as a soft, slow drizzle. When it's drizzling outside, the rain comes down in many tiny droplets that are hard to see. Some rain falls as a heavy downpour. Sometimes rain is even strong enough to cause a flood.

Precipitation brings water back to the soil, so the plants can take it in. It returns water to streams and creeks, too. The cycle is completed!

This little sprout needs rain to help it grow.

Snow and hail can cause **damage** if there's a great amount, or if ice chunks are very big.

Snow and Ice

Rain isn't the only kind of precipitation. If you live in a colder region, you might see snow. Snow is created when water vapor turns into ice crystals. Each snowflake has a one-of-a-kind crystal structure.

Sleet is precipitation in the form of tiny ice pellets. Bigger ice chunks that fall from the sky are called hail. Hail can be larger than a softball! It forms when upward drafts of air bring water droplets to a very cold part of the atmosphere. The water freezes and falls as ice chunks.

The Effects of Precipitation

Once precipitation hits the ground, it often soaks into the soil. Rain can change dry, cracked soil into rich, healthy soil. Rich soil makes it easier for plants to grow. When the soil has more water than it can hold, puddles form and even start to run off towards water sources, like streams.

The water level of small bodies of water, such as creeks and streams, may rise higher and flow faster. If snow falls in great amounts, it may add up to inches or even feet of snow.

This creek is muddy and higher than normal because of heavy rain.

We Need Water

A planet needs water to support life. The water cycle on Earth is important to helping plants grow, keeping **habitats** healthy, and **hydrating** people and animals. Some places on Earth have more precipitation than others, and they depend on a steady source of water. Deserts are areas that don't get much precipitation.

This toad relies on water for its habitat.

Each step in the water cycle is important. If there is not enough rain, then a place will experience **drought**. If there is not enough groundwater because of a drought, then evaporation and condensation may not occur for long periods of time.

Nature's Loop

Loops happen often in nature. The moon takes a certain path in the sky each day. The seasons change at the same time each year. Animals go through life cycles, in which they are born, grow, and give birth. You can think of it as nature's routine.

Natural loops help us predict what will happen. You know that it will rain if you see large, dark clouds. You know that puddles will form and creeks will rise if it rains too much. You know that water will evaporate if the air warms up. It's all part of the cycle!

Glossary

atmosphere: The mixture of gases that surrounds a planet.

damage: Harm. Also, to cause harm.

diagram: A chart, graph, or drawing that shows facts.

drought: A long period of very dry weather.

habitat: The natural place where an animal or plant lives.

hydrate: To add water to something.

marine: Having to do with the sea.

pore: A small opening on the surface of a plant.

series: A number of events that come one after another.

solar system: The sun and all the space objects that orbit it, including the planets and their moons.

Index